Mindful Digital Simplicity

Find your Digital Zen

Andrew William James

Copyright © 2024 Andrew William James

All rights reserved.
No part of this book may be reproduced. distributed, or transmitted in any form or by any means, including photocopying, recording, or other electronic or mechanical methods, without the prior written permission of the publisher or author. For permission requests, email cedar.place@icloud.com

CONTENTS

Introduction	5
Technology	7
Artificial Intelligence	11
How Technology has changed in your lifetime	17
Dopamine	19
Defining the states of Digital Users:	22
Digital Maximalist	22
Digital Denial	23
Digital Sceptic	24
Digital Minimalist	24
Digital Simplicity (Digital Essentialism)	25
Mindfulness in a Digital world	28
Computing Environments	34
Document Organisation	39
Cell Phones	40
Talking on the Telephone	47
Social Media	48
Digital Audio and Video Media	52
News	54
Work E-Mails	57
The Path to Mindful Digital Detoxification	62
Cellphones	62
Computers	64
The News	64
Morning Routine	65
Television	66
Music	66
Evening Routine	67
Hobbies	67
Listening with Intent	68
Ichigo Ichie	69
Introduction to the SHELVE framework	70

Introduction

Can you remember a time before digital technology played such a prominent role in our lives? Can you remember going on holiday and sending postcards to people at home? Laying on a beach with no cell phone or distractions? Taking a trip to the shops without being able to price check anything? Relying on printed maps for road trips?

Do you feel digital technology has taken over your life? Do you want to become less reliant on technology and more independent? Do you want to experience being off-grid? Is technology causing you to have feelings of anxiety? Do you feel your life is not as exciting or glamorous as the people on YouTube or social media?

Are you aware that there is not one moment of our lives that can be repeated? Each moment and everything we do every day is unique. We can never go back and relive moments, and we can never change the past but we can learn to make every moment count and by doing so enjoy our futures.

It has never been more important to understand the technology around us, how it works, who drives it, and the effect it can have on us.

With understanding comes the ability to make informed decisions.

It would be all too easy to abandon digital technology and isolate oneself in a cabin somewhere in the woods, but for most of us that's not an option and in any case there are alternatives.

Mindful Digital Simplicity (MDS) is not about abandoning digital technology, it is about taking control of it so that it enhances rather than complicates our lives.

Since the Digital explosion we have seen a rise in the number of people suffering and being treated for mental health and well-being issues related to anxiety, depression, exhaustion, ADHD etc.

Just as we thought digital technology had reached a plateau for a short while, Artificial Intelligence (AI) is emerging into our already cluttered world.

Even, now in its early stages, the lines between what is real and what is artificial are starting to blur. It is affecting nearly all spheres of life, information, news, videos, music etc.

It feels as if we are about to leave the Golden Age of information we can trust from legitimate sources and enter into a new uncertain age where the boundaries between reality and fiction are no longer quite so clear.

Technology

In its simplest terms, technology is the application of scientific knowledge for practical purposes, for example automation. Perhaps one of the earliest examples is the introduction of the Printing Press. This meant that written literary works no longer had to be reproduced manually.. Automation and printing meant that instead of writing by hand, copies of a work could now be mass-reproduced through printing blocks and a press. In 1476 William Caxton introduced his printing press in the UK. The first book to be printed on it was called "The Canterbury Tales". Other examples of early technology include harnessing wind and water power through mills, to drive equipment such as wool-making machines. Over one hundred years later and we are turning back to these early forms of power.

The Industrial Revolution brought with it, at least for people in the developed world, an end to poverty. Switching from hand making things to using machines meant that the process slowly became cheaper and safer. It raised the living standards of many people freeing them from arduous work involving hard labour. Machines started to do the hard work.

At the start of the Industrial Revolution, machines used renewable energies, primarily wind and water. At the time nothing else was available until the steam engine was invented, at this point machines became faster. As electricity became widely available they became faster still and ever more capable. Electricity facilitated the development of more inventions, radio, television, and communication equipment. Each invention paved the way for another. For example, the basic principles of television screens (cathode ray tubes) could be used to develop radar and later on computer monitors Each of these three separate developments led to advancements in their respective fields.

The early days of electrical or electronic technology were analogue.

The easiest way to explain analogue technology is to look at a vinyl record and compare it to a CD or streamed version of the same album. The vinyl record is analogue - its songs are physically converted from analogue sound waves into a series of continuous grooves onto first one side of a master disc and then the other side. This physical pressing is called a Master, it is pressed onto blank vinyl to create copies.

The digital version of the same album starts off as analogue sound waves. These sound waves are fed into an analogue-to-digital converter and changed into a digital file that can be saved on a computer hard drive.

The science behind it is converting the analogue waveform into a series of 1's and 0's that can be stored electronically. Once converted, a digital song can more or less instantly be transferred to another computer or made available on a streaming platform as it has no physical limitations imposed on it during the reproduction process. It is simply a digital transfer of information in an encrypted form which once decrypted gets turned back into music. In other words a digital-to-analogue conversion.

Playing back a vinyl record requires so many physical entities to be correctly aligned and the media itself to be free from imperfections, it therefore has its limitations and suffers from additional sounds introduced purely through the physical medium (i.e snap crackle and pops). Digital technology does not suffer from these inherent problems, however it is constrained by how much data can be stored and how quickly it can be turned from a digital signal back to an analogue one. The more data that is stored the clearer the sound or picture, however with more data comes the overhead of increased processing and slower transmission.

The move from Analogue to Digital technology really started in the late 1960s when transistors were invented. Without becoming too technical, prior to transistors we used tubes or valves to amplify audio signals in an analogue way. They needed high voltages to heat their elements and work, so they got hot, similar to an incandescent light bulb. These devices were used for all sorts of applications, including the first computers as far back as the Enigma machine.

These analogue components were replaced with transistors. They were much smaller, did not need as much electricity to drive them, gave off far less heat and were far more reliable.

The transistor revolutionised the production of a wide variety of electronic equipment, including radios, televisions, industrial computers etc.
Transistors were gradually replaced in the late 1970s to early 1980s by integrated circuits. These initially replaced tens, then hundreds and then thousands of transistors into one small chip.

From storage to processing data these 'chips' were able to store greater amounts of data and process the 1's and 0's faster and this paved the way to the development of electronic calculators, the first home computers and the first cell phones.

These electronic "chips" together with other electronic components are now being replaced with Surface Mounted Components (SMC) which are even cheaper to produce, smaller, much more powerful and use even less electricity.
Recently we have seen a revival of older analogue and some digital technologies, the increasing popularity of vinyl records and CDs for playing music, dumb phones instead of smart phones etc. There are many reasons as to why this is and many arguments to be had.

I believe it is because we are becoming more mindful of ourselves and those around us. Too much complexity has led to us being overwhelmed, we seek simplicity to restore balance in our lives.

People have always feared technology would steal their livelihoods but history has proved again and again this not to be the case. Old industries have simply been replaced with new ones. People have always had to learn new skills in order to survive and today is no different, or is it?

Artificial Intelligence

So far it has been relatively easy to define technology, however we now have a new invisible technology emerging, Artificial Intelligence (AI).
For a while, the science fiction stories of computers running the world and humans becoming their slaves were starting to look more like reality than the stuff of a writer's imagination. Fortunately, we recognise this new technology needs controlling. However, it does still represent a significant threat in what we perceive as being real and that which we may be misled into thinking is reality.

The Oxford Dictionary defines Artificial Intelligence (AI) as:

The capacity of computers or other machines to exhibit or simulate intelligent behaviour; the field of study concerned with this. In later use also: software used to perform tasks or produce output previously thought to require human intelligence, esp. by using machine learning to extrapolate from large collections of data. Also as a count noun (a type of noun that can be counted) an instance of this type of software; a (notional) entity exhibiting such intelligence. Abbreviated AI.

In reality machines cannot learn or think for themselves. However what they can do is process huge amounts of data very quickly and use that data to formulate an outcome.

Humans can manipulate the data to get the machine to give them their desired output.

Say I want to sell my car and I write the following advert:

For Sale, 2017 Volkswagen Golf, in good condition with 69000 miles and full service history. Two owners £X

If I ask an AI website, to process that advert and come up with something better this is what it produces:

For Sale: 2017 Volkswagen Golf
Price: £X

Details:
- *Condition: Good*
- *Mileage: 69,000 miles*
- *Service History: Full, meticulously maintained*
- *Owners: Two*

This 2017 Volkswagen Golf is in excellent condition and has been well taken care of. With a full service history and only 69,000 miles on the clock, it promises reliability and great performance. Perfect for both city driving and long road trips, this Golf is ready to go.

Features:
- *Comfortable and spacious interior*
- *Modern infotainment system*
- *Efficient fuel economy*
- *Smooth handling and ride quality*

Don't miss out on this opportunity to own a dependable and stylish car. For more information or to schedule a test drive, please contact [your contact information].

It does this by looking at other adverts across the internet searching for cars for sale, it then takes the format and phrases most commonly used in association with that model. But it does it very very quickly - in this case less than ten seconds.

If we try the same with a news story, for example:

Local MP has stated he did not eat an ice cream while driving his car along the M4 late on Sunday evening.

Run it through AI and we get:

Local MP Denies Eating Ice Cream While Driving on M4
[Your Town], [Date] — In a statement released earlier today, [Local MP's Name], the Member of Parliament for [Constituency], addressed recent rumours and social media speculation surrounding his actions late Sunday evening.

The MP categorically denied the claims that he was eating an ice cream while driving along the M4 motorway.
The controversy began when witnesses reported seeing a vehicle matching the MP's car make and model, moving erratically on the motorway. Speculation quickly spread online, with many claiming that the MP was distracted by eating an ice cream.

Addressing the issue, [Local MP's Name] emphasised, "I want to be clear that I did not consume any ice cream while driving. The safety of all road users is of utmost importance to me, and I always ensure that I am fully focused on the road."

Local authorities have confirmed that there were no incidents or accidents involving the MP's vehicle on the M4 at the reported time. Police have also stated that no formal complaints or reports were filed regarding the alleged behaviour.

Despite the MP's denial, the incident has sparked a debate online and in local circles about driving distractions and the importance of road safety. Community leaders have called for more public education on the dangers of distracted driving, while some have expressed their support for the MP, urging the public to respect his privacy and trust in his commitment to road safety.

[Local MP's Name] concluded his statement with a pledge to continue prioritising road safety and urged drivers to remain vigilant and responsible at all times. "My focus remains on serving the community and ensuring that our roads are safe for everyone," he added.
The matter, however, has left many in the community questioning the line between public scrutiny and personal privacy, as local residents continue to discuss the incident online and in local gatherings. The MP has reiterated his commitment to transparency and accountability, stating that he is ready to cooperate with any further inquiries to clear up any misunderstandings.

For now, the MP's office has asked the public to respect his request for privacy as he continues his duties in Parliament and within the constituency.
End of Story

In the above example it is very clear that commonly used news story phrases are being used. Some of it is clearly fictional since the original does not contain any witness statements. What is quoted is what in all probability the parties involved would say, in other words, stock phrases freely available in similar numerous reports across the internet.

What is worrying is that social media users are using AI to generate non stories that are not accurate in order to get hits and eventually earn money from such stories or videos. The stories appear and sound genuine but they are not.

You may also have heard of the term "click bait" this is where the author of a story will give you a headline that grabs your attention so that you click on the story. You read or watch the story as you are interested only to find out that it has nothing to do with the title.

Similarly you may be caught by headlines that tell you what you want to hear. For example your political party is wiping the floor with the opposition and looks set to win. You read or watch the story and it turns out it is just one person's view.

Video is another format AI is getting involved in to the extent that it can take a sample of the physical attributes of a person and based on video clips put together a whole new animated video as if it were the original person actually performing.

AI has actually been around for a very long time, although in the past we didn't call it AI. Take the AutoPilot on an aeroplane, it is called AutoPilot rather than AI as it cannot decide where it wants to go, it can only fly the plane based on a number of conditions being met and it does this very well. The Auto Pilot system cannot decide for itself a destination.

The Automated Assistants you may encounter on customer service sites, sometimes called Chatbots can be mistaken for AI, but in reality they simply recognise words in sentences and reply with standard phrases based on what has been programmed into them. A bit like a dog will pick out the word "walkies" in a long sentence and start wagging its tail (at the very minimum!)

What distinguishes humans from AI is that when we are unable to apply logic our decisions are based on emotions, feelings or intuition. Even when there is logic we are human and may still go with our gut feeling. AI can only make a decision based on probability and the data it is given it cannot act on instinct. If we decide to go against logic and emotion we may flip a coin or pick a straw, but this is a conscious decision and we will invariably override it if we do not get the result we want.

Mankind has reached a stage in its development where Technology has given us unrivalled choices in how we work and spend our leisure time and it is up to us how we adopt it. However, too many choices, too much information, uncertainty over what is real and what is fake, can create feelings of anxiety and affect our mental health. It becomes difficult to make choices and it becomes increasingly difficult to concentrate for any length of time.

How Technology has changed in your lifetime

Let's take a look at how technology has changed in your lifetime going back to the start of the Digital Revolution.

If you were born in the 1960s, or before, all domestic devices at the start of the decade were analogue, Television was limited to mainly terrestrial with little choice, and most most people viewed on black and white sets. Vinyl records, tapes and radio served as electronic audio entertainment. However, cinemas, concerts, sports, games, dances, reading, and playing musical instruments were very popular. You will have seen massive changes in the use of technology but will remember a time before cell phones, computers and social media. You will not remember being bored because of something that hadn't yet been invented or developed.

If you were born in the 1970s, your everyday electronic life will have started out mainly analogue. Television was just switching over from black and white to colour, vinyl records, tape or radio were the main choice of music, home computers were not available domestically and only just starting to make an impression in the workplace.

If you were born in the 1980s then you will have seen the emergence of digital technologies. In your childhood cell phones would have been dumb phones, Nokia 3210 etc.

The internet was accessed by analogue modems through domestic telephone lines and was excruciatingly slow by modern standards. The first widely available home computers, made by Commodore, Sinclair and in the UK Acorn hit the market around 1984. By the late 1980s to early 1990s Satellite Television became available, giving people more choice than the traditional terrestrial or cable television channels. Interestingly cable television came out as early as 1948 in America but was not seen until much later in the UK.

If you were born in the 1990s you will also have known digital technologies for your entire life. You will have seen digital technology get faster, cheaper and more widespread. At the start of the 1990s consumers were spending large amounts of money converting their libraries of Vinyl Records and Video Tapes to CD and DVD, only to be replaced again in a few years by online streaming services.

If you were born post 2000 you will have grown up with digital technologies throughout your whole life and it will be difficult to imagine a time before it. Digital technology affects nearly all aspects of our lives as we use it to work, live and play. Most of us use computers in one way or another at work, we choose what music and entertainment we want through streaming services and we spend more time socially interacting with others through apps.

Dopamine

Dopamine is a chemical transmitter or neurotransmitter made in your brain. It is used to help nerves within the brain communicate with each other, it also serves as a hormone sending messages to the rest of the body.

Dopamine plays a role in our behaviour, mood, learning, movement, memory, sleep, learning and arousal. When we do something we enjoy, dopamine is released and makes us feel good, it is a part of internal reward system.

So dopamine is good for us? Well like most things, in moderation it is. Dopamine is also released when we do things that are bad for us but make us feel good, for example eating junk food. The dopamine released makes us feel good after we've eaten junk food and the problem is we then want or crave more. In moderation junk food is enjoyable but too much of it can lead to health problems.

Too much dopamine will make you feel like your are on a high, you will feel energised and it is likely you will have a high sex drive. The downside is you will have trouble getting off to sleep, become more aggressive and act irrationally, you're likely to say things you don't mean. You are also at risk of developing obesity, addiction and mania.

Low levels of dopamine are likely to make you feel tired, demotivated, lacking in energy, moody, unable to sleep properly, have poor concentration and a low sex drive. Several conditions are associated with low levels of Dopamine such as ADHD, Parkinson's Disease as well as mental health issues like depression and schizophrenia.

If your brain releases the right amount of dopamine you are likely to have a greater sense of personal well-being, feel motivated, alert, focused and, most importantly, happy.
Part of the reason why people become addicted to alcohol or smoking is because of the dopamine that is released when they drink. It makes them feel good, but too much alcohol and we feel bad. If we are not careful we end up craving alcohol.

Studies have shown that it is just as easy for us to become addicted to social media, digital media and the news, as it is to alcohol. For example, the more likes we get to a social media post, the more we want to repeat the exercise and get even more likes from newer posts. Dopamine is released into our brains and in time, causes us to become addicts to social media.

The blue light that is emitted from screens in cell phones, tablets, computers and televisions affects the brain's ability to produce melatonin. Melatonin is the chemical that induces sleep, thus the release of dopamine coupled with a lack of melatonin means we have difficulty sleeping, which in turn affects our mood and behaviour the next day.

Manufacturers now recognise that the blue light emitted from screens can prevent us from sleeping and have introduced '" low blue light or cinema" modes. Whilst this will help, for example, if you are watching a film before bed, it won't stop the dopamine being released from a successful social media post. You will never see these low light or cinema modes being demonstrated in a shop because the image is dull and slightly yellow. Shoppers are looking for sharp, bright, vivid pictures.

In the past we didn't really have to worry about dopamine from media consumption as it simply didn't exist. Media was instead delivered in a controlled analogue format and without the social or communication aspects. Apart from deciding whether to listen, read or view there was no other interaction.

High levels of dopamine in the past were more likely caused by alcohol, gambling, risk taking, sports etc. Low levels may have been attributed to social circumstances, lack of money, lack of access to healthcare etc.

An emerging modern day threat to mankind are the diseases and behaviours caused by too high or too low levels of dopamine associated with the consumption of digital media. This can be overcome if we simplify our approach to the Digital World and become more mindful about our interactions with it.

Defining the states of Digital Users:

Digital Maximalist

This type of user as the name suggests uses digital technology to its maximum. They are likely, but not limited to, working in IT, Media or the Sciences. They are likely to be "early adopters" and participate in beta testing. More and more people are becoming digital maximalists as technology weaves its way ever deeper into our lives. A digital maximalist is more likely to stay abreast of new technologies, take pleasure in acquiring the latest cell phone, smartwatch, car and home entertainment system etc. They are excited by technology and there is nothing wrong with this until it becomes all consuming and takes over their lives. Thankfully most people do not allow this to happen to themselves.

Digital Denial

Whilst this is the opposite of the maximalist, this is not however a digital minimalist. To be in denial means you steadfastly refuse to adopt any digital technology whatsoever and choose to live off grid with no digital footprint. You don't trust technology and you refuse to try and see any of the benefits. You are sure you are right, even if not adopting technology causes you problems and inconvenience in your daily life.

The rather unkind, old-fashioned term for this is a Luddite. There are many YouTubers who extol a simple minimal off-grid life, yet, the contradiction is they are funding their lifestyle through social media and rely on technology to get their message out. In reality if you live a regular life - and by that I mean support yourself through conventional means and are part of mainstream society - your life will benefit from the use of some technology.

Supposing, for example, you decide you want to live a vintage life by adopting the values of another era and furnishing your home accordingly? You will still benefit from technology by being able to source items on the internet and meet other people who share your passion and interests through online communities. You can entertain yourself with a multitude of specialist vintage radio and TV stations covering just about every decade and every genre of music or film.

Digital Sceptic

As the name suggests there are some who are naturally risk averse, or sceptical. They tend not to be in denial but rather question technological advances and view them with suspicion. As with everything in life we need a balance. The sceptics amongst us, drive accountability and contribute to the overall safety of our digital environment through constructive criticism.

Digital Minimalist

These types of users, use digital technology in its absolute minimum form. They may choose a dumb phone in preference to a smartphone, they may use older technologies or operating systems. They prefer a minimalist environment with nothing surplus to requirements. A digital minimalist may, for example, prefer a tablet device over a laptop or desktop PC.

Of course there may well be some crossover between different categories and people are likely to stray between categories. For example, someone may have a dumb phone but use the internet extensively because of their work and therefore require a maximalist work environment.

Digital Simplicity (Digital Essentialism)

Digital Simplicity as defined by the author:
"Cutting out the unnecessary and unifying our digital tools to increase productivity and well-being"
So this is fairly self explanatory, it is about simplifying your digital environment so that you are free from distractions and able to concentrate solely on the task in hand.

By being able to do this we become more productive and when we are productively achieving our goals we have a greater sense of accomplishment and well-being.

Most of us already try to avoid distractions when we have a deadline to meet. How many times have you (or wanted to) lock yourself away in a room with no distractions to finish a piece of work? If you haven't been able to do this then the first time you do, you will find it empowering.

Digital simplicity relies on the user taking steps to simplify their digital world. There is no software package or app that can do this for you as we are all different. It requires **you** to take control of **your** circumstances.

By simplifying your digital environment you will naturally become more mindful. Digital simplicity is not about saying I will give up my smartphone, social media and never watch TV, it's about saying I will control <u>what</u> I watch on TV, <u>when</u> I use social media and <u>how</u> I will use my smartphone.

Three powerful words;

What, When and How.

What I will consume

When I will consume it and

How I will consume it.

Alongside that comes simplifying your digital environment so that unnecessary distractions are eliminated leaving you free to concentrate on the things that are important, like completing tasks. When you start the simplification process, you should also be thinking about what is the easiest way of achieving what it is you want to do. For example, if you just need a computer for email and access to the internet, then there is no point in spending lots of money on a gaming machine which would
have performance and facilities that simply aren't needed.

Whilst you're at it, why not look at the software on your machine and reduce it down to just email and internet access? This will eliminate distractions and save time on updates.

Another way of looking at this is to adopt the word Essentialism. By only using what is essential, you become a Digital Essentialist. This could be seen as extreme and would preclude some of the fun stuff!

In the 1990s I trained journalists how to use the new-fangled Microsoft Word 2.0 after we had migrated from Wordperfect (5.1). The Wordperfect screen was simple and easy to use with no icons. The operating system at the time, DOS, also had no icons. When we moved to Windows 3.0 everything seemed far more complicated and Word was full of icons that took some learning.

What we found was that the complicated environment stood in the way of productivity. We customised Word so that just the most common functions appeared as icons, i.e Cut, Copy, Paste etc. This was a very early example of Digital Simplicity. Removing the clutter and superfluous, removed distractions and allowed the user to get on with writing their article. An added benefit was that by just having icons that the user understood, the fear of clicking on the wrong thing was removed and confidence in the system increased.

Mindfulness in a Digital world

Mindfulness is defined as:

" "A mental state achieved by concentrating on the present moment, while calmly accepting the feelings and thoughts that come to you, used as a technique to help you relax"

So MDS is not a given tool, set of tools or hardware. It is more accurately described as a mindset that helps us simplify our use of digital technology so that it becomes a useful tool rather than a nuisance.

When we control how we use technology and use it as a facilitator or tool we naturally become more mindful. We are able to live more in the moment since there are fewer distractions. If you are in the cinema watching a film, it is unlikely you will have your phone in front of you and reply to text messages, so why do this at home watching the TV? If you have spent all day cooking a meal for your partner and they then pick at it as they are distracted by their phone, how does that make you feel?

In this digital world, there are so many distractions that we sometimes forget what it is like to just be in the moment and concentrate on what is going on around us, listen to what people are saying to us, enjoy the moment for what it is.

Why do we need a bluetooth soundtrack to our lives courtesy of headphones? Take the example of someone jogging across the sea front with headphones on, they're missing out on the natural, restful, calming and beautiful sounds of the sea and the seagulls. More importantly they can not hear the cyclists behind them or a bather in trouble.

Our time on this planet is limited, why complicate it with the unnecessary? Why not concentrate on what is necessary, productive and enjoyable?

In order for MDS to be successful it is important that the subject has the desire, need or want, to simplify their digital lives and to become more present in the moment, to enjoy life that is going on around them and become more grounded.

According to a UCL study published in 2023, there has been a sharp rise in anxiety since the year 2000 and within the age group of 16 - 24 year-olds it has risen two fold. Since 2011 the rise is more prominent in younger people with it falling off for those over 55.

Now there are many reasons as to why this could be and not all of it is digital related. Climate Emergency, Wars, Politics, Finance, Covid and of course the Digital Revolution giving us open access to everything at our finger tips. I believe part of the problem with the rise in anxiety is due to social media which has brought feelings of inadequacy coupled with restlessness and an ability to be quickly distracted making people lose concentration. In the author's opinion this can sometimes be misdiagnosed as Attention Deficit Hyperactivity Disorder (ADHD). In reality it is a case of being presented with too much choice, a bit like a child being let loose in a sweet shop.

There are numerous books and YouTube video, podcasts and articles extolling the virtues of shunning away from social media, smartphones and mainstream television. Right now there are reports of Generation Z reverting to typewriters as they find they can concentrate better on school/college essays. This is an extreme and in the modern world as unnecessary as ditching your smart phone for a dumb phone.

The mindset needs to find a mid point and change from "I can't live without digital technology", or "I will live out without digital technology" to "I can control digital technology". All it takes is willpower.

At some point or other in our lives we have all had to give up something or stop a bad habit. Every living being on this planet goes through some form of withdrawal process quite regularly.

Let's take as an example a diet. For you to lose weight you have to give up a certain type of food. Let's say for arguments' sake that the food is "chips" - you love the taste of chips and have them three or four times a week but they are stopping you from losing weight and you feel guilty every time you eat them. So, to lose weight you will have to give up chips until you are down to your desired weight.

At first it is difficult and you have withdrawal symptoms but after some time those symptoms disappear as you have learnt to replace the chips with something else that's healthier and doesn't make you feel so guilty. That could be eating an apple, banana or even sweet potato chips baked in an oven rather than fried.

Once you have reached your weight you treat yourself with a bag of chips, however at the back of your mind is how much better you feel for losing the weight, how difficult it was to lose it and so you end up having the chips once in a while as a treat.

So you haven't given up eating chips for the rest of your life, you have simply learnt to control when you eat them. If you walk past a chip shop and the smell of the chips is inviting you in you will have the willpower to say no and walk past. MDS is the same, it uses the same principles.

Twelve years ago an article appeared in The Guardian citing the observations of Bronnie Ware, an Australian nurse who spent a number of years working in Palliative Care. She recounted five of the most common regrets she had heard from patients in their last days:

1) I wish I'd had the courage to live a life true to myself, not the life others expected of me

2) I wish I hadn't worked so hard

3) I wish I'd had the courage to express my feelings

4) I wish I had stayed in touch with my friends

5) I wish I had let myself be happier

I interpret these observations as a case for using Digital Technology to enhance our lives but to remain in control.

If we examine each of these in turn:

Courage to live a life true to oneself

Influencers, content producers and those we associate with are telling us how to live our lives. To be truly happy and live a life of authenticity it is up to us the lives we choose to lead. We can use Social Media to learn certain skills or to help us form opinions.

I wish I hadn't worked so hard

Being in online and available 24x7 will do you no good in the long run, switching off is Important. Whilst earning money is important to enable the pursuit of dreams, it should not come at the cost of your health or well-being. As sure as paying taxes, when you are gone someone else will take your place.

I wish I'd had the courage to express my feelings

Whilst you can do this in the online world, there is nothing as rewarding as expressing your feelings in person to someone. Sure you can express your feelings in a text or email but in person carries with it romanticism. Debating something in person can be more productive and enables us to perfect listening skills. It also ensures that if we do say the wrong thing or cause offence we can backtrack before any damage is done.

It is easier to communicate with clarity and passion in person. Digitally there is nothing to stop us giving a thumbs up or down to express our feelings. If you do feel strongly and passionately about something in an online debate then don't be afraid to air your opinions, just be aware that everyone may not share your viewpoint and that once expressed, your opinion maybe there for eternity.

I wish I had stayed in touch with my friends

Through sites such as Facebook, it is relatively easy to re-establish and stay in contact with people. Digital Technology means we can meet virtually and communicate instantly. With that ease comes a certain amount of laziness and it is easy to fall out of communication with people as there are simply too many ways to keep in contact. Whereas in the past we would arrange to meet every so often or have a "catch-up call", now because we see the person on our social media or as a "logged in" icon, it is easy to leave that catch-up until another time.

What really matters is staying in contact with friends who reciprocate your friendship and with whom you have a quality relationship. As with most things it is quality that matters not quantity. What is the use of having 250 social media friends if you never get to talk to them or meet them in person? Surely it is better to have 10 really close friends who you regularly message, meet or talk to than 250 periphery friends?

I wish I had let myself be happier

To a certain extent happiness relies on being authentic, if you cannot be honest with people about who you are, what you believe in and what makes you, you, then what chance to do you have of forming meaningful friendships and being happy?

Letting yourself be happy is something we can all do if we simplify our lives and make room for what's important by shedding the unimportant. In terms of digital simplicity it means ditching the things that provide us with no value or connection to the real world.

Computing Environments

Digital Simplicity focuses on using technology but simplifies how it is used to achieve better productivity, focus and user experience.

A good example of digital simplicity, often mentioned in a computing environment is the Apple ecosystem.

Because Apple control the hardware and software environments, the user experience is consistent, there is less chance of something not working as it has been written for Apple-specific hardware. But it is not perfect and the same experience, depending on the software you are using, can be had from hardware and software on the PC/Linux/Android platforms.

An example of where the Apple ecosystem may not work in a simple environment is the users need to retain the same experience across personal and commercial data environments. In this instance to simplify the digital experience the user may have to decide which digital office environment they will work in or accept that they may have to learn two different systems.

To decide on the model you are going to adopt, it is worth spending some time initially reviewing the level of integration you need between different hardware and software environments.

Many companies insist their employees use equipment supplied by their IT department as it can be monitored, controlled and encrypted. In this scenario, you have no choice other than to have two systems, but if you are self-employed or work freelance you may have that choice. As more and more companies opt for cloud based systems, the need for company issued equipment may start to decrease with users choosing and purchasing their own hardware.

As previously mentioned, where equipment is supplied by your company, you may find it simpler to use the same applications on your own personal equipment. In the past, I had to use one system at work and I found it easier to buy a copy of the same software for my own machine. This saved me having to learn two different systems and avoided incompatibility between systems.

Alongside writing and coaching, I also use computers for my amateur radio and flight simulator hobbies. Even with so many different requirements it is still relatively easy to simplify my digital environment and remain productive.

To begin simplifying your digital environment, draw up a list of all the tasks you need to perform on a computer, tablet or phone. Include both personal and business tasks.

The table below shows the applications I use for different tasks, the type of hardware and the percentage of time I spend using a particular type of device. Some applications are hardware-specific. When drawing up your own table, you will most probably want to include the operating system and hardware manufacturer.

	Personal / Business (P/B)	Computer	Tablet	CellPhone	TV Streaming
% of Use		70	5	5	20
What	*When*	*How*			
Task					
Word Processing	PB	Y	Y		
Spreadsheets	PB	Y	Y		
Diary Management	PB	Y	Y	Y	
Email	PB	Y	Y	Y	
Document Storage	PB	Y	Y	Y	
Music	P	Y	Y	Y	Y
Photographs	P	Y	Y	Y	Y
To Do List	PB	Y	Y	Y	
Notes	PB	Y	Y	Y	
Amateur Radio Echolink	P	Y	Y	Y	
Amateur Radio Slow Scan TV	P	Y			
Flight Simulator	P	Y			
Video Streaming		Y	Y	Y	Y
Video Meetings	B	Y	Y		

Having decided what your tasks are, where you need them and on what hardware you are going to use them, you can now decide which applications you will use for those tasks.

An important part of this is to research which supplier has applications compatible with the hardware you are using or want to use.

Where to store your data is another consideration. There are many solutions currently available on the market, from storing them in the cloud to storing them on a USB stick.

Your choice may be influenced by where you need to access your data from. Do you need to access your data on the go and on different devices or do you just need to access it from one location and on one machine?

The table on the next page may help to determine your own software requirements based in the operating system you are using (i.e Windows, IOS, Linux etc) In the example below I use everything on an operating system that is compatible with my personal and business software and hardware requirements.

	P/B	Computer Operating System 1	Computer Operating System 2	Tablet	Cell Phone	Streaming
% of Use			70	5	5	20
What	*When*	*How*				
Task						
Word Processing	PB		Y	Y		
Spreadsheets	PB		Y	Y		
Diary Management	PB		Y	Y	Y	
Email	PB		Y	Y	Y	
Document Storage	PB		Y	Y	Y	
Music	P		Y	Y	Y	Y
Music Storage	P		Y	Y	Y	Cloud
Photographs	P		Y	Y	Y	Cloud
Picture Storage	P		Y		Y	Cloud
To Do List	PB		Y	Y	Y	
Notes	PB		Y	Y	Y	
Amateur Radio Echolink	P			Y	Y	
Amateur Radio Slow Scan TV	P					
Flight Simulator	P					
Purchased Films and TV (Stream)	P		Y	Y	Y	Cloud
Video Meetings / Work System	B		Y	Y		

You may find that you use a mixture on different operating systems.

Having taken stock you are now ready for the next stage which is working out how to simplify things and incorporate mindfulness.

Ideally when working across different digital environments you should be aiming to have as close to the same experience on all machines with everything looking familiar. The list below provides some tips:

- Use the same colour scheme and desktop background

- A blank background helps you concentrate on the task in hand

- Delete any software packages you don't need

- Delete or disable widgets like weather and news apps, these will just distract you

- Keep your desktop clean with just shortcuts to the applications or documents you use every day

- Make sure you are storing documents in a location that is backed up and accessible from other devices should you need to be able to access them on the go

Document Organisation

Wherever you store your documents it is desirable to have a filing system that is simple and allows you to find documents easily.

Perhaps the best way of thinking about how you store your documents is to view storage as a hierarchy. At the top level, you have the location where your files are stored. This could be locally on your computer's hard drive or in the cloud.

Where you store your files is up to you. I store my work documents separately from my personal documents in two separate cloud locations. Within each cloud area, there is another hierarchy based on the type of file.

So, work files for example have four high-level directories – Projects, Information, Documents, Archive. Within each of these, I then have further directories for each project. The Archive folder serves as a place to store everything I have finished with. By keeping the number of high-level directories low and expanding within lower levels you create a system that is easy to navigate and easy to store files in.

Take some time to think about your directory structure, can you reorganise it better? Your directory structure may be fine as it is and you just need to have a tidy up.

Always keep an archive folder to store any files you don't use now but may need in the future. As storage is cheap you can always set yourself a 5-, 10- or 20-year rule to keep files for.

Remember that some workplaces will not allow you store to documents outside of their own systems due to legislation or governance requirements.

Cell Phones

Cell phones used to be a simple device we used to make phone calls and send texts. They were convenient tools and most people felt excited about getting their first cell phone.

As time went on the devices started incorporating games, then cameras and finally internet access. As technology became cheaper and more readily available the devices firstly shrank in size and then became ever larger and more powerful as they became capable of performing tasks more readily associated with computers and tablets.

As prices came down some users found it necessary to carry around two cell phones, one for work and one for personal use. Others simplified and just carried the one cell phone.

The main problem with cell phones is that we are contactable all the time. In recent years the devices have taken on the role of our personal portable digital hubs with email, social media and all sorts of other applications competing for our attention.

If you use a cell phone for work then personal calls and texts will distract you during working hours and if you have a work phone then you will be distracted in your personal time unless you switch it off or setup "do not disturb" time zones.

We reach for our phones when we are bored, feel lonely, out of habit or guilt that someone may need us.

So how can we start controlling how we use cell phones? Well perhaps the best place to begin is with starting to control feelings of guilt. Unless you are on call or expecting news of an important event you do not need to feel guilty about not answering a call, text or email straight away. The world will not stop and everyone drop off the planet because you do not answer an email in your own personal free time. Your time outside of work is time you have to yourself. It is the time your body and mind have to recover so you can work productively the next day.

Some people I've seen, think that by replying to emails at eleven o'clock in the evening they are showing how keen and hard working they are. They are not. What they are showing is their own insecurity and their inability to manage their time effectively.

The same applies to taking business calls during your private time or responding to texts.

If this is a scenario you struggle with then try applying the "**W**hat, **W**hen and **H**ow" principle.

What: Work, Emails, Phone Calls and Text

When: During working hours only

How: Either a separate cell phone which is switched on only during work hours or I will only respond to emails from my computer rather than on my phone and I will divert work calls to voice mail out of hours.

Many cell phones allow you to create groups of callers and implement focus times, blocking those groups of callers. For example you may decide to create a group called Friends and block calls from people in that group whilst you are at work or driving. Similarly you may have a group called work and only allow calls from the group between 9am and 5pm Monday to Friday.

The same "**W**hat, **W**hen and **H**ow" principles apply to social media, do you really need it on your cell phone? Why not just look at it on your computer? Do you need an app for the news? Why not catch up on the news once or twice a day at a time that suits you?

Once you start looking at the Applications on your cell phone and think about the amount of time you spend checking them for updates, you begin to see where your time is going.
It has become popular recently for people to take a Digital Detox. In its extreme form this involves, at great expense, locking yourself away for a few days in a cabin in the woods with no access to a cell phone or the internet. Whilst this might make you feel good for a few days, it is not the answer as you are withdrawing from everything in one go and it's just too much of a shock. Much better to cut down slowly.

There are applications that can simplify your phone and make apps available during certain times, but these are likely to get out dated and are no replacement for you deciding for yourself how you will use your phone. They are also no substitute for willpower! It is doubtful that they will provide a long term solution.

To start simplifying your cell phone life ask yourself:

What information do I need to access?

When do I need it?

How will I access it?

It's worth bearing in mind that before you go cold turkey, you may not need to delete apps completely, you can always hide them from your main screen.

On my cell phone, I decided that I wanted it to be as simple as possible. I use an iPhone as it integrates seamlessly with my computer and iCloud where I keep my documents, calendar, notes and "to do" lists.

Using the original spreadsheet of what I need and where I need it, I looked again at the iPhone column and added in some extra lines that are specific to that device.

	Personal / Business (P/B)	iPhone	Computer
What	*When*	*How*	
Phone Calls	P	Y	
Text Messages	P	Y	
Diary Management	PB	Y	Y
Music	P	Y	Y
Photographs / Camera	P	Y	Y
Notes / To Do Lists	PB	Y	Y
Banking	P	Y	Y
Satellite Navigation	P	Y	
Apple Wallet and Store Cards etc	P	Y	
Train Journey Booking App	P	Y	Y
Car Parking App	P	Y	
Weather	P	Y	
Browser	P	Y	Y
Facebook	P		Y
Access to Documents etc			Y
E-Mail	PB		Y
Amazon	P		Y

By deliberately deleting social media apps and email I have no need to check my phone other than a couple of times a day.

Removing Amazon has made me think more about whether or not I actually need to buy something straightaway or if it can wait till I am at my computer and had a chance to consider the purchase.

When I had finished the exercise I was left with the tools I found useful and that I would have found inconvenient not to have access to.

I have considered having a dumb phone and did in fact try one for a few weeks. However, my car doesn't have satellite navigation which is fine until you need to go on a long journey and require traffic updates. My camera is an SLR and far too big and heavy to carry around everyday. Other reasons are listed below:

Nearly all supermarkets seem to want you to get a loyalty card and offer discounts if you have one. To take advantage you either need to physically have the card on you or have their App. I have the Apps for all the stores I am likely to go into but have put the cards into the Apple Wallet so that I can just open the Wallet App and choose which store card I want to use. The Apps themselves are hidden from view.

I use the Apple Wallet App for paying for things using contactless technology. To me, the fact that it requires a fingerprint seems more secure and I can keep my cards at home. If I lose my phone I can just block the phone but still use my bank cards.

Being able to check my bank account balance on the go is invaluable, it makes it easy for me to control my spending and know how much money I have (or don't have) at any given time.
The TrainLine App is great for buying discount train tickets and storing them in the cell phone.

Similarly the Car Parking App makes it easy to pay for parking, especially as the parking machines either don't work or are very complicated. I get a reminder when the end of my parking time is due and I have a receipt on the phone as proof of payment.

The end result is that I have a simplified phone that does what I need it to and is a tool. It saves me having to carry lots of clutter. All I need to take with me when I walk out of the house is my cell phone and the lack of social media and email means I can get on with enjoying what I am doing.

I will be the first to admit that keeping your cell phone simple does take willpower and I do still sometimes contemplate moving to a dumb phone in the future. You may find the same as you progress along your digital detoxification pathway.

There is no right or wrong way of detoxifying it is up to you how you progress and things will change, you may find that you want to become more extreme as your life changes. For example when I retire I can envisage a life without a smart phone, but now is not the right time for me personally.

The end result is that I have a simplified phone that does what I need it too and is a tool. It saves me having to carry lots of clutter. All I need to take with me when I walk out of the house is my cell phone and the lack of social media and email means I can get on with enjoying what I am doing.

Talking on the Telephone

Sometimes it is difficult to remember that the primary function of a cell phone was originally to make and receive phone calls. With so many people emailing or texting or Whats Apping it is easy to forget the art of actually calling someone.

I found a useful solution from a company called Xlink (available on Amazon). They sell a device for around £70 that uses a Bluetooth connection from your cell phone and connects it via a wired connection to a normal landline telephone plugged into it (corded or cordless).

With landlines being phased out, this device allows you to use your old landline telephones with newer technology. More importantly, you feel more present when talking to someone on a landline telephone and there is no way of being distracted by pings on your cell phone from apps.

Social Media

If you are engaged in social media you have to accept that sometimes things may not always go as you want, resulting in your well-being and happiness being affected. There have been many stories of teenagers suffering from depression and anxiety as a direct result of posts on social media. Bullying can be indirect and commonplace, whether intentional or not.
Social media, when used correctly, can be a great source of entertainment, discovering new interests and staying in contact with relatives, friends and our local communities. However, used incorrectly it can be destructive and leave us with feelings of inadequacy.

There are obvious social media platforms such as Facebook, Instagram, and Twitter. The less obvious platforms are Television, Radio, WhatsApp, and Magazines. All of these have one thing in common. They try to show or influence us how to live our lives. They do this through images and stories of people they think we should aspire to be. It doesn't stop at celebrities, sometimes friends and relatives also seem to want to let the world know how well they are doing and what fantastic lives they are leading. They want the world to know how wonderful everything is for them, they want the likes, praise and adoration. This is how they get their dopamine hit.

There is a need in society to be seen to be doing well. The reality is in "keeping up with the Jones's" today we are depriving ourselves of the futures which will make us happy tomorrow. If we are constantly seeking the next best thing we will never enjoy what we have today, now and in the future.

The word "luxury" has never been so overused as it is today. TV programmes and social media are overrun with people leading luxury lifestyles, driving luxury cars, and wearing designer luxury clothes.

All of this is of course entirely possible and achievable if you prioritise spending your money on these items above everything else. Even if you can't afford to buy them outright, you can have most "reasonable" things through a subscription-based service or you can max out your credit card. The problem with subscription or leasing is you never get to own the items, and in both cases someone somewhere is making money out of your desire to have the things you want today.

The question you may want to ask yourself is do you want to be the person that is influenced by the influencers or do you want to be your own person and do things your way?

Controlling your social media engagement is no different to any other form of digital simplification, If we look at Facebook, for example, an approach might be:

- Decide what it is you are getting out of Facebook, why are you using it, who do you want to keep in contact with? Unfriend people you no longer want to keep in contact with or do not bring anything positive to your life

- Decide which groups you want to be involved with, which groups make you feel positive and which groups annoy or irritate you. Leave the groups which are not bringing anything meaningful to your life

- Look for groups aligning with your interests as a way of replacing the groups of people you are no longer interested in

- Limit your time looking at Facebook. Cut back slowly at first before eventually checking in two or three times a week

- Remove the Facebook app from your phone if it is installed and just use it on your computer

- Think twice before posting on social media. Is what you are saying accurate, will it cause harm, are you happy for the world to read what you have said? It takes two seconds for someone to copy or forward a post and it is then on the internet forever. Think twice, send once

- Try observing rather than contributing, see how this makes you feel

- Be wary of connecting with people from the past. Most of the time it can work out really well, but sometimes it can be disastrous - think twice, they may not be the person you remembered them as. Don't be afraid of unfriending them if you have doubts

- Never post pictures when you are on holiday. Thieves and scammers can easily find out your address and will know your house is empty. The same is true of placing "check-in" flags when you go out to a new restaurant or meet up with friends. If you want to tell your followers where you are, wait till after the event and you are home

- Think twice about any pictures you post online. That new watch may be your pride and joy but what if people start questioning how you can afford it?

- Stay safe online, never give out your address, phone number, licence plate or any personal details

- Don't worry about leaving groups or unfriending people, it's your life to live the way you want to live it

- Experiment with deactivating accounts rather than deleting them if you are in two minds

A by product problem with social media is that it can leave a footprint of who you are and things you may have said in the past, may come back to haunt you.

If you are thinking of applying for a job, be aware that some prospective employers may try and find out more about you before or after your interview by looking you up on social media. It is therefore important for you to clean up your social media image so that it presents the person you want your employer to see.

If you have a lot of content that could be considered inappropriate in any way either remove it, or, temporarily hibernate your account. It totally depends on how much you want the job and if you are prepared to compromise your authenticity.

An option worth considering is to restrict who can see your accounts. Remember if you are not careful with your privacy it is not only an employer that can see what you post but your friends, family and associates.

Now might be a good time to either quit social media or delete your account and start again with a new one reflecting the new you!

Start thinking about:

What social media do you want to take an interest in? Will it benefit you? Which people or groups do you want to be connected to?

When will you consume or participate in social media? Once a month, week, day or set times in the day?

How will you consume or participate in it? Your computer, tablet or phone? If you are serious about controlling your exposure to social media then look at it on your computer maybe at lunchtime.

Digital Audio and Video Media

Not so long ago our choice of audio and video media was extremely limited. In the UK we had a handful of terrestrial TV channels delivered in an analogue format through the airwaves. If you wanted to listen to music then you listened to a whole album on records, cassettes or a compact disk. There were no streaming services, satellite TV was in it's infancy offering a handful of channels at great expense. On demand didn't exist, everything was distributed through analogue channels with limited ways of consuming the content. For example you could only watch television programs and films on a TV set (or projector if you were wealthy enough) Radio was delivered on the radio and records played on a record player or recorded onto cassettes if you wanted to take your music outside your home.

Now we have a vast choice of the media we consume. For a monthly subscription you can have access to a library containing nearly every album ever recorded. Similarly with films and TV programmes from all over the world. Books can now be delivered to you digitally. You have the choice of what you consume, when you consume it and how you consume it through a variety of digital devices giving you access to audio, video, books and more.

For some of us it has become common place to flick through the hundreds of TV channels and content on streaming services, play a film for 10 minutes and move onto the next one. The same with music, we listen to maybe a couple of tracks and then move onto the next album. We have become intolerant of content we don't like, it has become easy to dismiss something as rubbish if we don't immediately like it.

In the same way social media creates feelings of anxiety, envy and restlessness, so too can instant access to content, unless, you control how you consume it.

Most of us understand that if we have four bottles of wine in the house and drink all four we are likely to feel ill and won't have enough wine left to enjoy another evening unless we go out and buy more. Digital media allows us to stream as much content as we want,.You can never run out and at the end of the evening there is still more available the next evening. The problem is the vast quantity makes us every hungry for more, eventually fostering feelings of restlessness and discontent.

Recently there has been a huge increase in the sale of vinyl LPs. The difference between listening to an album on a vinyl LP against listening to it through a streaming service is that it is not so easy to skip to the next track or album, you end up listening to one side of the album all the way through. You become more aware of the music, it is easier to put your phone away and concentrate just on the music. The same analogy holds true with video. If you watch a DVD you are more likely to sit and watch it all the way through.

In both scenarios you are consuming media with intent, you have chosen the media you want to consume and are more mindful of the content.

When you are streaming music from your phone it is far easier to get distracted with the phone and text, email or use social media whilst listening to the music. You are not concentrating on the music and therefore not fully engaged and getting as much enjoyment from it had you sat down with the intention of listening only to the music.

Rather than switch solely to analogue formats for media consumption, why not instead consider consuming with intention. Set aside time to watch a film and don't be tempted to channel hop or flick over to another film. Do your research, compile a list of films and programmes you want to see and set your own schedule. Pick out programmes on TV you want to watch and note down when they are on. In other words create your own TV schedule that is full of content you are interested in and that will entertain you.

If this works consider taking the same approach with music. Decide what you want to listen to, when and how. Allow time to discover new music but in the main if you want to be entertained then listen to what you know or is recommended by friends. The idea is not to restrict yourself but to not waste time and energy consuming media that doesn't give anything back to you.

For both Audio and Video the intention is to listen or view in the moment. That is to be present, without distraction so that you can enjoy the work as the artist intended.

What will I listen to or watch?

When will I listen or watch?

How will I listen or watch?

News

Until relatively recently, most of us listened to the news in the morning on the radio and a main news program on television in the evening. We find ourselves exiting the Golden Age of news and entering a new era. News is now available 24x7 and on any digital media platform you care to think of.

I spent seven years working for a TV news station in their IT department. We covered a 24x7 shift rota. Mounted high up on the wall of our office was a speaker which constantly delivered the news. This could be a car crash killing ten people or a political event. Whatever the news announcement, it was never good. I would say less than 5% was good and very infrequently would it be uplifting.

This was at the start of 24-hour news coverage in the UK. The news programmes would mainly repeat themselves during the day. Little has changed since then.

Look at YouTube and you will find hundreds of channels reporting the news. Some of which is based on hearsay from social media, the reporters own assumptions or how they've interpreted the News from traditional sources. The stories are presented in such a way that they give the impression of being corroborated, researched and investigated. You will find that some videos will be titled in a way that makes them appealing and makes you want to click to watch. Sometimes videos will be long winded and will not contain anything useful.

For example " X (a celebrity) denies robbing a bank" They may not have robbed a bank but are being asked if they have to make a juicy news story that will attract views and ultimately earn money for the channel.

Quite often stories are speculation of what could or may happen. When it hasn't happened, it is forgotten about. The downside is that someone somewhere will have spent hours worrying about what could or could not happen. A recent example of this has been the massive meteor shower from the Sun that could have hit the earth – nothing happened but it got people worried unnecessarily.

Others from the turn of the century featured the millennium bug. We were led to believe planes would drop out of the sky, there would be a major crash in the banking world, and there would be general pandemonium all over the world once we were a second into the Year 2000. Nothing happened because the IT industry worked hard to ensure these sorts of disasters wouldn't happen.

More recently Artificial Intelligence has just started to influence the news, with fake stories, quotes or videos appearing causing more speculation and at worst, panic.

The most impartial news stations I've found are those that the left wing call right wing and the right wing call it left wing.

We can debate the news and worry over it, or we can choose to limit our exposure to it. By limiting our exposure to the news, we are clearing our minds of distractions, allowing us to concentrate on what's important, rather than worrying about things over which we have no control.

If you manage to miss the news for a couple of days, you won't have missed much and not much will have changed. Either whoever was being hounded to resign has resigned or the episode has blown over.

If you feel anxious because of the news then you need to ask yourself three questions:

What news am I Interested in? At home, abroad, science, sport, politics or just general news?

When am I free to follow it? In this way you can limit your exposure to say the morning or in the evening.

How am I going to catchup with the news? Will it be online through a website, an App on your phone (not recommended if you are trying to limit your phone use) or on TV?

Alongside this will be who you choose to be your news provider, by limiting yourself to one or two providers you trust, you are more likely to control your consumption of the news and reduce the possibility of suffering misinformation through AI.

If you find you are being affected by the news try intentionally not consuming it on any platform for 24 hours and see how this affects you the next day. This is in a way a news detox, albeit on a limited scale. If you find this is successful and your emotional state improves, gradually cut down your consumption to once or twice a day from trusted providers.

Work E-Mails

It is customary for us to leave out of office messages on our work email when we are on holiday. Usually this is along the lines of:

I will be out of the office between x and x. I will respond to your email on my return.

The problem with this is that when we return from leave we find we have hundreds of emails to read and respond to. Then there are the never ending trails, most likely by the time you start reading them they will all be out of date. You may spend hours playing email catch-up instead of getting up to speed with what's been happening whilst you've been off.

You have a few choices. One is to delete all the emails sent to you whilst you've been away, if it's important they will get back to you. You could, on the other hand, just read the latest emails as they will be the most relevant and delete the others, or you can spend hours going through them all.

Another way of dealing with the problem is for it not to be a problem. Instead of the traditional email why not leave something along the lines of:

"I will be on leave between X and X, any emails sent to me during this time will be automatically deleted. If your query is urgent please contact X"

Of course this may not be practical in all circumstances but if you talk to your work colleagues you may find it beneficial for everyone to adopt this kind of stance.

Think about how much better it would be to have a face to face verbal catch-up with your manager or your deputy when you return rather than trawl through emails and lose your enthusiasm on your first day back at work.

Another problem I have noticed in the workplace is the perceived requirement to immediately respond to an email.

Some view this as a way of showing others that they are working hard and on the ball.

I used to sit in meetings with, say, fifteen other people all reading their emails on their phones, tablets or laptops. It was quite clear they weren't listening to what was going on and were more obsessed with their email. They were not in the moment and certainly not paying attention, the result being that meetings went on longer than they should and were not productive. I am still not sure why some individuals think they are presenting a positive dynamic image of themselves by not listening to what's going on around them. Not only is it rude to the chair of the meeting but it's rude to everyone around the table.

If you are unsure on a response to an email or need to gather facts first, don't be afraid to put off responding and wait until you have gathered your data and are clear on what you are going to say. Your email will be coherent and factual. If you need longer, send a holding statement stating you are looking into the matter and will get back to the sender in due course.

At the other end of the scale are people who do not respond to anything they don't like or that they think may trip them up.

Usually this is because they don't have enough background or knowledge to respond. If someone asks you a question then it is common courtesy to respond with a reply, even if it is a holding statement. If an email doesn't require a response from you, for example you are copied in for information, then there is no need to reply. Similarly if you haven't responded to an email and the subject matter is out of date then there is no point in replying.

Whilst we feel we are in contact with people through email it can lead to feelings of isolation since all our business communications are through this medium rather than by actual talking or video conferencing. Instead of replying to a complicated question and ending up with a large email trail why not ask the sender when they are free to discuss. In this scenario both you and the sender have each others' full attention, you have time to consider your response and if the subject is complex or politically sensitive there is less chance of miscommunication.

The same principles apply to Whats App, texting and other forms of instant or direct messaging.

I have found that allocating time during the day to deal with emails really useful. I know that I will be responding to emails for an hour in the morning and an hour in the afternoon, the rest of the time I have my email closed so I can concentrate on other activities. This makes me more productive as I am able to fully concentrate on what I'm working on rather than get distracted with email. I will also sometimes switch my phone off so that I am fully engaged in what I'm working on. The upside of this approach is that whilst you can only concentrate on one task at a time, you are fully engaged in it, it will be completed quicker and will be of better quality.

You may have heard the phrase "Deep Work", this is a phrase coined by Cal Newport in his 2012 book "Deep Work: Rules for Focused Success in a Distracted World". In it he describes the activity of "Deep Work" as a "professional activity performed in a state of distraction-free concentration that pushes your cognitive capabilities to their limit. These efforts create new value, improve your skill, and are hard to replicate."

A first step towards reaping the benefit of deep work is adopting the mindset of eliminating or reducing distractions so that you can fully concentrate on the task in hand.
We all want to be able to multitask but we have one brain and one pair of hands and can only be in one place at a time. Rather than time share my resources I allocated them to one task at a time. I wouldn't for example be able to coach someone while responding to email and writing a paper. It wouldn't be fair to the client and it would add unnecessary stress into my day as I wouldn't be able to respond properly.

Finally, as mentioned earlier, unless you really need to, there is no need to look at or respond to emails outside of working hours. The same is true of personal email. If you want to reduce stress and anxiety, schedule a time to look at your email and make sure this is not first thing in the morning when you wake up!

Applying the rule of What, When and How

What emails shall I reply to?

When will I reply? Does it need an immediate response or do I need to gather data?

How will I reply? Will I reply by email or will I call the sender so that I can deal more fully with their query?

The Path to Mindful Digital Detoxification

Going cold turkey, with any addiction, rarely works unless you have super human will power.

You have a few choices, one is to go away for a few days and rent somewhere that doesn't have wifi or cell phone reception. This, whilst nice, may not be practical to most people, so you are left deciding which steps you can reasonably take, when you can take them and how you can take them.

Cellphones

The device that we probably look at the most during the day and have on or about our person all the time, is the cellphone. Statistics vary on usage, but various surveys report the average user checks their cellphone approximately 60 - 80 times a day. With users spending on average four and half hours on their devices, that's over one day a week or seventy days a year spent looking and interacting with a cell phone. Starting your digital detox by gaining control of your phone is therefore the best place to start.

Start by clearing down unwanted Apps, delete social media and spend a few evenings a week keeping your phone in another room while you are watching TV or listening to music.

Unless you are waiting for an important phone call or need to have a cell phone on you for medical or safety reasons, try going out without it. Spend some time reflecting on how that made you feel? The first time I did it I felt liberated! We do not need our phones on us at all times, if something goes wrong find someone to help you. If you are using your phone to pay for things then try taking cash or a bank card with you. Buy an alarm clock and remove your cell phone from your bedroom. If you need to have it close leave it somewhere handy outside your room. This will remove the temptation to check it before going to bed.

A constant source of surprise to me, are the numbers of people going to the gym but spending most of their time looking at their phones and in doing so hogging the equipment! I spotted someone earlier today spend at least ten minutes on one machine whilst he was texting, then relax on the machine for a further five minutes waiting for a reply presumably.

If we engage in activities then we are never going to to get the most out of them by having our phones on us all the time and interacting with them. With bluetooth headphones there is no longer any need, and with that any excuse to have your phone out in the open when at the gym. Now you can use the time to either concentrate on the exercise with some music or simply concentrate on the exercise without music.

Some of us feel we must multitask the whole time, we don't realise it's OK **not** to multitask. The moments we have to ourselves are precisely that, they are moments for us to reflect and enjoy being with ourselves and the person we are. They can be thinking moments and a time to consider decisions we are making. They do not need to be seen as wasted time that needs to be filled with listening to a pod cast or learning a new language.

Computers

Now lets turn our attention to your computer"

- Remove unwanted software and applications

- Clean up your desktop

- Organise your files

- Clean up your browser

- And the final electronic detox is social media

    - Take stock of the sites and groups you belong to. Do you need them? How long do you spend on them? Are they giving you anything worthwhile in return? Having cleared social media Apps from your phone the next logical step is to either delete/suspend your accounts altogether or review your use. Social media can be fun but don't let it become a distraction.

The News

Now it's time to tackle the news, again. Look at **W**hat, **W**hen and **H**ow.

What: What news do you want to hear?
When: Do you need to hear the news first thing in the morning when you wake up or can it wait until later in the day?
How: Identify a source or sources of news you trust and limit your consumption.

If you find the News is upsetting you or too distracting then don't be afraid to cut back.

Morning Routine

Establish a morning routine. For me this is the most important part of the day. When we wake up we need to be hydrated and wake up slowly. If you meditate, now is a good time to do this before the day gets started. Maybe go for a run or to the gym. If you enjoy cooking then start the day with a healthy, nutritious breakfast.

Early morning is the ideal time to plan your day. If you are working, set time aside for dealing with email, block out time to complete tasks and don't be afraid to take yourself off line while you are completing them. Even if you are not working it's still advantageous to have a plan of what you are going to do. If there are jobs you have put off doing for a while, now is the time to schedule them in, or perhaps you deserve a day out somewhere? It's your day, plan it and enjoy it, just don't waste it.

If you find you do not have enough time in the morning, set yourself a goal of waking up earlier.

Television

Start thinking about how you can "mindfully" incorporate television into your life. Initially maybe allocate one evening a week to watching a film you've always wanted to watch.

You could invite friends or family round for a film evening that is cell phone free or simply enjoy it on your own.
Next start considering the programmes you want to watch as opposed to just watch because it is something to do. Ask yourself the questions: what are you getting from watching TV? Is it enriching your life? Could you be doing something else instead?

Music

As with television try doing the same with music. One way of being more mindful and present whilst listening to music is to use headphones, just make sure your cell phone is not in your hand. Close your eyes and just listen to the music. If you are outdoors and it is safe to do so take in what's going on around you, does it enhance your soundtrack? Observe people, most of them will be looking at their phones! Appreciate nature and the beauty of music. Practice mindfulness.

Evening Routine

Establish a weekday evening routine. Life would be pretty boring if every evening was the same, but establishing an evening routine when you have work the next day will help you wake up refreshed and ready for the next day.

Try and introduce a break in-between finishing work and cooking dinner or settling down in front of the television. Do something completely different like going for a walk, cycle ride or anything that gives you that separation between work and your evening. After dinner work out what you are going to do that avoids jumping straight onto social media. Get used to no screen time half an hour before bed, avoid caffeine and sugary drinks.

Whatever you do it should be a time for you to unwind from the day, relax and prepare yourself for the next day. It is particularly important to introduce that break time if you are working from home.

Many of us, during the COVID lockdowns, got used to finishing work, eating and then jumping straight back onto our computers to socialise or continue working. In the long term this is damaging since it does not allow our minds time to switch off, relax and reset.

Hobbies

Hobbies are so important to our well-being. A hobby can be anything you're interested in, so long as it distracts you from the digital world. Reading, writing, running, going to the gym, playing a musical instrument or even join a local club.

Listening with Intent

Stephen Covey famously said: "Most people do not listen with the intent to understand; they listen with the intent to reply."

As you start to remove the digital surplus in your life and become more mindful of your digital interactions, you will begin to notice that life will naturally start to slow down. You will begin to find you have more time to listen more closely to what people are saying.

Listening with intent is something we should all strive to practice. If we listen to reply then we are not listening. We are simply thinking about what our reply is and our brains are concentrating on formulating that rather than listening and then thinking of a reply. If we are only listening to reply we are robbing ourselves of the opportunity to learn. We only learn by listening and sometimes we can learn something new or even change our minds. Listening with intent trains our minds to become more receptive and open minded.

To train yourself in this practice, begin by pausing before replying to someone. Give yourself time to reflect on what they've said, then reply.

Ichigo Ichie

In the opening chapter of this book, I mentioned that every moment in our lives is unique, this observation comes from the Japanese book of Ichigo Ichie. The book details the art of making the most of every living moment. It is something we should all think about. Do we want to skim through our lives or do we want to enjoy our lives with passion, meaning and intent?

If our intention is to ensure we enjoy our lives and the moments within them then we need to recognise that acknowledging and savouring the good times is as important as learning and moving on from the bad times.

Once you start mindfully adopting digital technology you will find new pathways in your life opening up. Enjoy each step of your journey and appreciate the benefits.

Nothing is easy but if we want more meaningful lives and to live as individuals we need to recognise what's holding us back and act accordingly. Sometimes, when we want to change, others around us don't want us to change through fear that they will lose their partner in crime, they will do their best to try and talk us out of our plans. At worst they will ridicule us for wanting to improve our lives. If you want to change your smart phone for a dumb phone then do it, don't be afraid of what others think. The only person that will be against an alcoholic giving up alcohol is their drinking buddy.

Introduction to the SHELVE framework

If you have enjoyed reading this book and wish to look at improving other areas of you life, you may be interested in my book called SHELVE: Scandinavian Lifestyle Habits.
The SHELVE framework is based on my own experiences and is a collection of what has and hasn't worked for me.

The idea of SHELVE was born from taking six key life areas and fusing them with six facilitators or tools to find a framework that could help people get closer to achieving happiness and well-being.
 The six key life areas are Hobbies, Health, Home, the Environment, Social and Economics. The six facilitators or tools are Slow Living, Hygge, Lagom, Improv, Vintage and Simple Living.

hobbie	S	low
healt	H	ome
hyyg	E	nvironment
social	L	agom
impro	V	intage
simpl	E	conomics

Interestingly the number six in Feng Shui represents "flow". In certain Chinese cultures, it represents happiness and blessings. Many businesses will display the number six to invite good fortune and wealth. And in numerology the number six signifies domestic happiness, harmony and stability. All of these are principles and beliefs of the SHELVE methodology.

SHELVE is not just a list of six life areas and six facilitators, it is more a fusion of the two and why the categories are broad. Each area has an interdependency on at least one of the facilitators. So, for example Economics, or Finance can be influenced by any of the facilitators, in that, when the basics are right there is space to live a Simple, Slow or Vintage lifestyle. However, a Simple, Slow or Vintage life will help with getting your finances under control. The same is true of your home, once a home is decluttered there is then space to do what you want with it and follow your style.

You can find SHELVE on Amazon and other online bookshops in both digital and print formats.

www.ingramcontent.com/pod-product-compliance
Lightning Source LLC
Chambersburg PA
CBHW030454220526
45464CB00006B/2541